EFFECTIVE SAFETY TRAINING

The SIX STEPS to create
a successful
SAFETY TRAINING MANAGEMENT
program.

©2017 Edgar Fernandez

Content

Introduction

These are the reasons that motivated me to write this book. The first question is, why don't employees and workers apply the knowledge that they have learned in training? Second, why don't employees and workers speak up during the training sessions? What I observed during my experience is, why don't employees and workers participate very enthusiastic to develop and improve their safety management programs? With the fourth question, which you're going to see in the first chapter, why are we still having a high number of losses, incident claims, and fatalities in Canada? With these outlined reasons, they have an answer. That's the reason I divided this book into two parts. I'm in favor of leadership. Leadership is very different from being a manager. Being a leader doesn't mean that you're in the top position to manage as a vice president, presidency, or director.

A leader is supposed to make the people better day-by-day. That's the second leading reason for the questions that I mentioned, which prompted me to write this book. As I said, leadership is critical to training on a level of any safety management system or trying to introduce a process safety culture; you need to develop your leadership. You'll need to learn how to approach people, have conversations and accept criticism. How much you are able or capable of failing because of every situation that safety presents during your professional life. You're going to fail, but the question here is, are you going to become better after that failure? That's the reason why I'm bringing this book. That's a problem that many safety professionals of any safety management programs in the inner city haven't worked. According to, he's a leader I'm coaching now in the United States.

He has said that North America has a problem of leadership, and I agree with that point. The numbers that I mentioned in the first chapter reflects that. Here's how you can develop a leadership as a safety professional and how you can become a better trainer in safety management. There are a lot of materials now on social media or the internet, such as podcasts, consult and blogs, with people writing articles about many safety topics and in which training is one of them. The reasons why there is a failure in practice is the lack of leadership. Second, we don't apply the methodology, and the philosophies of the adult training have. In this book, I mentioned earlier how you're going to set up a training program. What are the learning principles? How to develop goals and objectives. How to implement the training program. How to prepare the training material. How to follow up the training.

I mentioned concepts of coaching and mentoring. Those are very important to apply in training. Last, I am Edgar Fernandez. I have 22 years of experience as a safety professional and as a professional engineer in the pharmaceutical, chemical, food, and oil, and gas industries. I urge t you to apply the knowledge of this book that I'm willing to share with you through these pages, and you're going to succeed in your safety management program. You're going to can influence other people because at the end; trust is the most important thing as a safety professional or as any professional. Leadership is the other one. You can influence people to work safer. In the end, that's the mission. My mission is to protect people's lives and reduce Incidents by consulting and training. Thank you very much. Enjoy this book.

Part 1
The Current State of Safety In the industry.

According to the Association of Workers' Compensation Boards of Canada, there have been 232,639 lost time claims and 832 fatalities at the workplace in Canada in the past year, 2016.

The industries leading the claims are the manufacturing, Health and Human Services, construction and retail trade. The manufacturer and the construction sectors are also driving the fatalities claims too. The national recordable lost time incident rate was 1.51. However, some provinces in Canada have the rate above 2.00.

In the United States, OSHA, the Occupational Safety of and Health Administration released a pre-report of the top ten safety violations of 2017, in the middle of September this year. By the way, this ranking hasn't changed at least for ten years.

The number one safety violation is fall protection. General requirements according to the OSHA regulation 1926.501, they have issued 6,072 citations to the industry.

The number two safety violation is hazard communication or HAZCOM. According to OSHA regulation 1910.1200, OSHA has issued 4,176 citations of these safety aspects, hazard communication.

The number three safety violation is scaffolding. OSHA regulation it's 1926.451. OSHA has issued 3,388 citations.

Then number four is respiratory protection OSHA regulation 1910.134. The number of citations issued by OSHA had been 3,097 citations.

Look out, look out, it's the fifth safety violation in the industry. The standard that we need to follow, it's the 1910.147. OSHA has issued 2,877 citations for these safety violations.

Number six, ladders. OSHA regulation is 1926.1053. OSHA has issued 2,241 citations for these violations.

Powered industrial trucks, OSHA regulation 1910.178. OSHA has issued 2,162 citations.

Machine guarding, OSHA regulation, 1910.212. OSHA has issued 1,933 citations.

Number nine, is fall protection for now in the training requirements? According to OSHA regulation, 1926.503 number of citations issued by OSHA, have been 1,523.

The last one, number 10 is electrical wiring methods, which is standard 1910.305. The number of citations issued, 1,405 by OSHA.

The question is, do you believe that the efforts of the industry have been enough to provide these rates or these numbers? As we can see, the numbers reflect that our safety strategies have not been effective.

They are still high. One fatality is too much. We cannot tolerate these anymore. In my 24 years of experience, I have seen the industry have waste, defecting the safety program only by one indicator. The [Lost Time Incident Rate], the LTIR. It's through this indicator LTIR, which affects the state of your safety management system. However, there is a lot of work to do behind the scenes to keep this KPI below one.

The next question is, do you know there are other KPI's you need to make sure that or track your safety management program or keep the LTR below one, as we are aware of managing the effectiveness of supply chain in the organization?

The management establishes between five to 10 KPI's. These indicators are crucial to track results on saving, managing of materials and people resources. The government and industries only rely on the LTIR. Therefore, we do not manage safety according to the management principles.

We ask our workers to report hazards because we demand them to identify at least one per month, per day, per week depending on the vision of the company or needs of our clients. Therefore, we believe that incidents will decrease because everybody thinks about safety and it's better to be safe. However, we still have high numbers lost time claims or even worse fatalities.

It's in the workplace safety that has gone through areas of developments since the beginning of the industrialized revolution.

- Number one is an inspection error.
- Number two, the unsafe conditions.
- Number three, the industrial hygiene.
- Number four, the noise.
- Number five, the safety management.
- Number six, OSHA.
- Number seven, the accountability.

Number eight, the behaviors based on humans. It's essential to understand them to build a robust and inclusive safety management program to reduce occurrences and have strategies also to decrease the numbers that I mentioned before.

Some companies have matured their plans to get to the current era, that is behavior based and human. That means a program, which makes everybody part of it. Currently, in the industry, a few companies are at this stage. Many of them are on the OSHA or safety management. Then, another bunch of companies is still on the noise or in the inspection area, that which is the first era. That's even worse.

It's imperative to understand people in our workplaces to feel a successful safety program. Take account of the following aspects; Number one, workers need to find motivation in the program. Number two, how and what we are going to communicate with the program that includes expectations, goal, and objectives? I shared the information communicated that is relevant to the workers. Build a safety attitude. That means we might not to know what attitude means and how it can be transmitted. For these aspects, leadership has an important role. There are some experts about this topic in social media or books to learn about this fascinating subject.

Also, there are training programs in specific institutions and universities. Our consultants specialize and have a lot of experience on this topic. However, leadership is something that you don't learn in two, three or five years. It Includes the following characteristics; life experience, work-based experience, maturity, and wisdom. The most important and the last one but not the least is to be able to make people better than before and yesterday or even better than you. That may be sacrificed for something to make others better. That is important in safety because of people and workers, have the position, or they can have that belief that once you demonstrate or they can learn the role of leadership, it will make your safety program more effective and efficient.

One of the critical components that will detect a part of success is to communicate expectations. The question is how? The answer is simple, manage the problem. There is a well-known program named Total Quality Management, [TQM]. Edward Deming is considered the father of Total Quality Management. Some companies hold the triple certification, which means they manage quality, environment, and safety through a very well-established management program. Organizing this type of analysis through their equation between workers and angles of the business, that is required teamwork.

Chapter 1
People's Involvement to Succeed in Safety

I elaborated this chapter on people's involvement to succeed in safety.

In the first episode, we described the current state of safety in the industry in Canada. I talked a little bit about people.

In this section, I intend to share my experience on how to build the safety attitude. It's almost, but the question is how? Well, I want to share my personal experience, and I have used lean manufacturing techniques such as Kaizen for the recent years, for the last five years.

Organizing this type of analysis will clear a cohesion between workers from all angles of the business, this requires teamwork. Also, allowing the participants to develop a plan to improve the safety of the specific task, we create ownership, a sense of belonging, confidence, and empowerment. These characteristics are essential for safety.

The role of the safety expert is to support the team by answering their questions with regards to the regulations, the standards and other information and tools requested. Using lean manufacturing techniques such as Gemba Walks creates a sense of ownership as value. They are the starting points of the various learning experience designed to help participants better to understand the role in creating safety thinking through the lean safety management. Led by their behavior in taking a walk. These walks need to be structured to provide focus and a methodology to be performed by using the scientific method called Plan, Do, Check, Act, [PDCA].

This methodology provides a deep understanding of the causes of every problem, which can only be achieved through direct observation of work processes and the fact-based information which comes from people who work in these processes. More information can be found in many books, such as Jim Womack's latest book, Gemba Walks. Communication is a key to have a successful safety management program. Therefore, there is another lean manufacturing technique called the Kanban Boards. Kanban is a tool in lean manufacturing to map the process of finding bottlenecks to reduce waste and other issues, but any even project that requires inserting safety into business. It would help them to find hazards and their potential outcomes by hazard assessments.

Hazards cannot be eliminated at all but can be controlled in the following order. Eliminate, substitute, administrate and PPE. Follow the PDCA, Plan, Do, Check, and Act to determine an action plan and publishing to the Kanban Board. It will give all the worker's a sense of ownership, a feeling of belonging and motivation to keep supporting safety. Also, the organization shall post these assessments, and plans need in the executive Kanban Board sometimes called Tier 4 Board, where senior managers and directors review the progress and resources given.

In this chapter, I want to talk about the role of the senior leadership team members that are critical to the implementation of any management system or initiative. In my personal experience, 50% is how we involve employees into the safety program. The other 50% is support from senior staff. You can find more information about how important the top leadership teams support the staff initiatives.

Lean safety applies many principles of lean manufacturing to improve the communication of expectations. That could be one of the most significant gaps in the program. People always want to be communicated about how new initiatives are progressing, how they can participate in expressing new ideas or interacting with other issues. Using the key performance indicators, which gives room to direct communication, not speculation. Communication performance of the program provides us with some data to adjust and improvements and also creates a sense of ownership and belonging to all the employees to make the program better.

Firstly, I would wait to before I start measuring your safety management program by getting lagging indicators. At this stage, we will identify the weaknesses.

Secondly, create the leading indicators to build a path where the program should be.

Thirdly, establish the transformation indicators. To measure the thoughts of your employees in the program, it's essential and in recent years trust for people has been a critical component to the success of any initiative in any company or business. The reason why it's vital to measure or to create transformational indicators.

Through my experience, I have seen 98% of the companies consider their incident break down as the most important indicator to measure its performance. As we see in chapter one, according to the numbers from the Association of Workers' Compensation in Canada and the pre-report released by OSHA, well, that is not enough. Then, also I expressed my agreement and disagreement on why we need to have more KPI's.

As I said, there is a lot of work to do on having these indicators that will help the business to achieve their ultimate result that keeps your employees safe from injuries, managing assets, and reducing production lost time.

Chapter 2
Basic Ways to influence Behaviour and Accountability

Safety professionals or leaders can influence behaviors to have successful management programs in the following way. To change attitudes in the belief that our behavior is consistent with our attitudes. Number two, to build a psychological climate in which people will choose to behave as they wish since the action helps to satisfy their current needs. This is called motivation. Once the employer has given all the tools to the employees, the employees will start looking for better strategies to achieve goals safely and efficiently.

Number three is to modify their behavior through the systematic use of reinforcement called coaching. Following that practice, we also influence the future responses as well. In safety management, we call it "safety approaches." However, we tend to forget point number three. We concluded the job when we delivered the message by training, safety talks, communication boards, etc. However, we don't do the follow-up that is called coaching to assure that employees have understood the message and give them the appropriate tools to perform a specific task. It's essential to follow the cycle plan, do, check and act. In my experience,

I have found that some organizations are struggling with accountability. How many of you as safety professionals have heard, "Safety is the responsibility of everyone" or "safety is the number one priority". Personally, I have heard both several times. However, I found the statements partially true, because of the following reasons. Number one, with regards to these statements they are the goal. Accountability is the key to lay out a successful safety program. Through these years in safety, I have identified that the meaning of the word accountability is different for each manager, vice president, director, operator or supervisors and safety professionals.

Having different perspectives of accountability becomes a problem. New companies that believe in multi-disciplinary teams, the members are accountable for their specific role in the group. The simple reason is to avoid micro-managing and promotes growth. Some international companies that are operating in the base behavior safety area they have defined correctly the roles of players that are involved in safety ranging from the president to the contractor and to the visitor level in the environmental and safety policies to avoid the following. Having different opinions of who is responsible and accountable for this or that will lead to blame and pointing fingers. It promotes terrible relationships between all employees and doesn't promote leadership, it fosters distress and increased incidents.

Safety professionals or the leadership teams need to analyze if the accountability exists or not in the company to be successful in safety. Some factors are always the key to make the programs, which depends on how successful it is in businesses or the industry nowadays.

The number one reason why the safety program does not excel is due to lack of promotion and prioritization. Many of the safety programs s with a safety-first statement. This type of approach generates an orientation to build a safety organization that separates the production instructor, rather than create safety into the regular system and activities.

Also, it creates conflicts in the first line of supervisors, middle, and upper management in the position of making choices between safety and production every day, hour and minute. We know who's going to win. Yes, production. Why? Adopting this approach, it forces the people to place priorities all the time between safety and production. Consequently, we are in a win-lose situation battling for priorities. By building in safety, we can put ourselves in a win-win situation. We don't force managers and supervisors to make all these choices. Therefore, we must obtain safe production that will push ourselves to plan, design, maintain and follow-up all activities built-in safety.

For example, including safety in the protocol of designing a new equipment or workstation or in the process of management of change that is in modification will help to establish a process of decision making without prioritizing between safety and production.

Number two, communication and motivating. The traditional safety programs attempt to communicate with our people, to motivate them, to change their attitudes without trying to modify their behaviors. The standard tool that we utilized are videos, posters, booklets, signs, displays, bulletin boards, banners, slides, and others. Are they effective? We don't have the data to support if they are useful or not. But having said that, it doesn't mean we cannot use them. It is imperative to analyze data that are created to have a fundamental understanding of its effectiveness.

The number three is training. Traditional safety program depends so much on training. We spend much money on buying, build safety training programs, videos, slides, and other tools.

Also, we spend an enormous amount of time on training experience on new employees, because of the legal requirements. Is the training program effective? Have the needs of the position and staff been analyzed? Has it changed the behavior of the employee? Frequently, we have a regular program in a reading fashion because of the law. Coaching is paramount to conduct and verify its effectiveness. In my opinion, it's the most important activity that a professional safety manager or front-line supervisors must do to build trust and change behaviors.

Number four deals with building hazards. We routinely put workers in a situation that they remain trapped or we put them in workstations to perform tasks where logically and physically their actions will lead to cause some injuries. Most of the incidents investigations suggested that the employee was careless or he or she did not use common sense. Common sense is different for everyone. Common knowledge is the same for everyone. We are still relying on common sense. Human factors are the real hope to fix this type of issues.

The number five is inspections and records. We have spent a considerable amount of time on conducting inspections to comply or demonstrate [inaudible 00:38:05] before government authorities. However, we don't take time to analyze the data they produce to identify trends. Records have the same ending; they go to the document storage area to be in the archives of the company.

Number six is the tradition. The society is changing our areas that we have seen before in technology services, communications, except for communication. We are still using the same traditional methods to educate people. Companies have safety concerns to solve every day. However, we always try to find solutions using the conventional ways. We don't use managerial techniques; we manage safety as we do to plan forecast and execute production. We are very competent to control costs, waste, return on investment. Manage the complexity of the projects, but not safety.

Why do we use those techniques for safety? We tell workers to stay passive, to execute procedures and then, they don't participate in hearing them. We do not allow them to be active to solve their problems. As human beings, we like to be independent. We don't want somebody give us orders or instructions that we need to do our job. It's our nature. To start making safety programs, we need to start promoting participation. We need to allow our employees to participate more in safety projects. That input based on real experiences can occur on the floor or workstation. As a leader is known as a manager, we need to recognize that they have more experience than us. Why? They are exposed and educated in this task every day. Therefore, they have great ideas to solve safety problems. Employee centered leadership needs to allow employees to find their solutions. As managers, we provide the knowledge on regulations, codes, and standards. Job enrichment is the number three option. It allows them to participate and find answers that will feel valued for the job and the company.

Chapter 3
Safety Management-Path of Success.

Although, OSHAS 18,001, the CSA Z100 in Canada are the same. The OSHAS safety and health management system is regularly updated to robust the management program in the last 20 years. Companies are still facing challenges such as incidents that could have severe outcomes as a result. Also, the OSHA 1910.119 personal safety management is changing to risk-based process safety, [RBPS] for the same reason. All these management systems have a common enemy that is called involvement, this will lead to the highest level of safety performance. Safety perception elite, will help to have a very successful program. Analyzing these requirements from the management point of view, it has two perspectives. First, management. Second, leadership.

Management and leadership are not the same concepts. I want to start with a simple definition of these two words according to the Webster's Dictionary "Management is the act or skill of controlling and making decisions about business, department, sports, teams, et cetera". They are the people who make decisions about business, office and sports teams. Third, the act or process of deciding how to use something. The process to plan, do, act and check, [PDAC]. It belongs to this concept, there are other components such as the definition of goals and objectives, developing programs and strategies as well. Definition of leadership "is a position or leader of group organizations, etcetera". It is the time when a person holds a position of a leader and power or the ability to lead other people.

As we can see, this definition of leadership is not a position such as a manager, it can be but it's not a must. Frequently, we confuse this word with being a manager automatically. We believe that we have become leaders right away. In the past I agree, nowadays I disagree. Leading people requires a lot of maturity, training, experience, values and being brave to challenge that school. In one of the articles from Forbes, it talks about leadership. Leadership has always been and will be the most asset on the Earth. Without it, no amount of money, resources or talent will ever achieve sustainable success for any organization. But with it, other odds and obstacles can be avoided. Leadership is what moves us from point A to point B. Leadership is what makes each of us all, and gives us the potential to be fresh. Leadership is what gives us hope for a better tomorrow. No one ever said it was easy to follow this process to become a more effective leader.

Lead yourself first. The most important person and most difficult person to lead will always be yourself. It is the [inaudible 00:45:30] that will require most discipline, commitment, and determination. However, it is also the aspect that will repeat the most significant rewards. One of the most effective methods of leadership is to lead by example. Everything in an organization starts with a leader, the temple. You said it would generally set the tone for how members within your group interact with each other, as with others outside your organization.

It is a double-edged sword. It can be a significant influence over career and a positive mentality within your organization. However, you can lose your temper towards an employee or a contractor. Don't be surprised when one of your employees decides that this might be acceptable for him or her to do the same towards a colleague. There is no simple and fast rule here. Not only should one know the difference between what is right and what is wrong, but you should be practicing it and lead your words every day. As a leader, you have 24 hours by seven. By the time you need translations, conduct yourself with the same level of discipline and maturity that you expect from others, and you will get it.

In the article of Forbes August 6th, 2012, you can find it on the internet. In conclusion, these two characteristics are demanding to be satisfied with the implementation of safety management programs. Especially, in a very dynamic environment with a mix of people and generations. In conclusion for part one of this book, these two characteristics have demanded to be successful in the implementation of the safety management program. Especially, in a very dynamic environment with a mix of people generations. Currently, employees always like to know the facts or the reasons to perform or conduct a job in a certain way. Then, they will feel motivated to excel and have the benefit of his/her career and once they think that as part of their project, his or her contributions will be significant.

PART 2
Safety Training Management Program.

According to the preliminary report from OSHA in the United States of the top 10 safety violations in 2017, the ranking hasn't moved or hasn't changed since 2003. In reviewing what the common findings have been in these citations, training is one of the common factors on why OSHA has given these fines and warnings in a citation manner. Nothing has changed since 2003. We are talking about 14 years of these top 10 list of safety violations. You see the first time to report you know only the citations, then, you do your research and investigate the content of the citations. You start seeing that training is a significant component of that violation. Therefore, this part two is essential for this book.

Nearly everyone recognized the valiant efforts of the workforce training. It needs to be done correctly. Training can make workers efficient and effective. You can increase production, revenue, and profits. Also, you can save cost, waste, and inefficiencies. Training can lead to increased compliance with the regulation. That is the problem nowadays in the industries. They believe that organizations only train people they think are going to comply with regulations, but it's false, because proper training, effective and efficient training is part of the system to have an excellent safety management program. Compliance shouldn't be the end of the result, it should be part of the system.

One of the problems nowadays. We need to establish systems, instead of saying, "We train people, we're going to comply." It is partially right, but it's not everything. When we listen to answers such as we comply with safety, we'll have a good safety program. We don't have any problems. We are 100% in compliance. Those are the type of answers that I have heard or listened to from managers, CEOs, vice presidents of many companies. That means you are in trouble with that kind of responses.

I don't want anyone to misunderstand me that training is not essential. Training is critical. However, we cannot say that it's training for those who are going to comply. It's part of the system, it's something that needs to be measured, and that's the reason why there's a part two of this book. There are other elements in the safety management program or quality management system. If there is a need to interpret everything that you need to measure, it will make an efficient and effective training program or training management system, then, you're going to be on the path of success on managing your management system in your company.

The benefits of the training can lead to having a happier satisfied workforce, which reduces turnovers and costly onboarding, so the benefits are many. Creating a training management system that sometimes is called effective training isn't easy. These are common problems, including creating training that doesn't support our real business world. That's the reason why I was saying that training shouldn't be only for compliance because it's more than that. You need to find out the business call of providing that training. What are you going to achieve by delivering working heights and training? What's going to be the business impact of the training? We know by the fact that you're going to comply, and you'll establish the working heights for example. These training programs are calling for the regulations, but that doesn't mean you meet.

Also, we believe that training programs can fix problems, but that is not true. It's more than that. To fix issues you'll need to have specific mentality approach to fix them. It's not only training. Without identifying the real purpose of the training or that which includes too much information, maybe all those things, they may become a problem. The question here is, how does one get effective workforce training materials? In the next page, we're going to talk about the eight steps that can help you to create efficient training materials.

Chapter 4
Steps to create a Safety Training Program

The first step to decide on a safety training program is to conduct a much-needed assessment. For example, in one of my previous works, it was a workstation, a production line that they had, had many Incidents in the last three years. They needed to find the solutions in the production line to stop these incidents, that went from near misses up to reportable, one reportable incident. The production manager and the manufacturing director approached me, and they asked me what type of training program we can design to be more efficient and stop these incidents. Before anyone rushes off, creates new materials, you should assess the situation. The whole of the training needs assessment.

There is a need for training assessment; they include the following; need to identify the precise business goal that the training supports. In this case, would you want to reduce the events or improve production? What's going to be the business call for this training? We need only to tackle the safety part of the training for that production line. We need to address all the training, with all the aspects included in the production line. Then we found, because we used lean manufacturing and that we needed to tackle all the production line training program. Also, we need to determine the tasks the workers need to perform so the company can reach the goal. You need to make an inventory of works of each operator at each position in the production line and how they perform. From checking defects, up to setting up the line to start up on Mondays for example.

What's going to be the activities we help them to learn so as to perform the task. One of the things I actually want is to make a stop on this one. In this step, we have seen a lot of changes nowadays through technology. Through generations, there is a generational change, or a generational behavior change nowadays. Technology changes too fast. We have more things we have access to more information. It has become more quickly; therefore, we can be updated many times and still have the most updated information. However, the only thing that has changed in 100 years is the way that we educate people. That's a problem, because if technology change, the way that people are getting access to that information will likely change. The idea of how we perform our activities has changed drastically in the last five years, and education hasn't changed in 100 years, that is where we have a problem.

Adults claim that they like to learn, to experiment and to put ideas to see whether the work or not. That's one of the things in our industry needs to think about and learn learning. Alvin Toffler, a futurist who wrote a theory " The Third Wave Society" what describes the role of knowledge and technology in this era. He describes knowledge as the fuel of progress whereas technology is its engine. He urged the need for both individuals and societies to learn ways to adapt to and manage the sources of over-rapid change.

We have seen many fatalities and many lost time incidents. The lost time incident rate keeps increasing; it's still too high in some provinces here in Canada. We have seen the top 10 safety violation hasn't changed for 14 years. It means our training shouldn't be all about having people sit in a classroom, having an excellent PowerPoint presentation and have an expert talking and answering questions. We need to change that in a way. We need to promote the learning process. They need to learn by themselves like playing with Legos and let them experiment. Until then, the piece is a sample and that's what kids do, and by so doing they learn learning. Adults are not different.

The most significant issues in training that haven't changed the ways to train people. We need to determine the characteristics of the workers that will make training more effective.

I want to tell you a story. I volunteered with a food bank here in Bradford Ontario, Canada. Now one of my colleagues, another volunteer is a disabled person. She is blind. She performs her job very capable, very efficient. For me, it was an open eye experience, a good experience, because how are you going to train people with those characteristics? Everybody has a right to make a living. Everybody has a right to have a job. You put it in a manual work like this. This person is doing the manual picking and placing food in boxes.

I was observing my coordinator the way t she was training her; for me, it was new because what they told me when we started that day was, "This person is here." I was in shock because I didn't have experience before to train a blind person, but the coordinator came, and for her, it was easy. It was something fascinating to see that maybe you might have in your facility and what you're going to train people like her to be safe, to make the job safer. It's fascinating. What type of characteristics do your workers have?

You have a population of workers in a specific production line. You need to ask how they want to learn, what their characteristics are. Some of them like books, some like PowerPoint, others want to be on hands projects, etc. You need to make them think to find solutions.

The solution should come from them, not from us. We need to direct this group of people to find the answers. That's the thing; you need to determine the characteristics of the workers. That will make the training more effective.

Maybe, we need to create some new material or a podcast or something, that's going to add value to them as well. You never know, because you never ask. That's a problem as well. You need to ask. You need to interact more. We need to see how we can change this educational system methodology. Sitting, putting them in a classroom as I said and somebody talking in front of them I think hasn't been sufficient for now, and the numbers show that. You still see that on the safety violation list, training has been an issue.

Summarizing, you need to have a clear view on what is the business goal and how you're going to support. You need to have a list of tasks that they are performing on that specific workstation or job. You need to help them to learn how to perform those tasks safely. You need to know the way they want to learn. Also, by doing that, you're going to determine the characteristics of learning of the group. Now I'm going to explain a little bit more on these four steps.

The first one is, you're going to identify your business goal. Don't provide training if it's not clear on what you are doing and if it doesn't have a direct support of your business goal. You need to relate each one of the training to what the business is doing. I'm going to put something simple like working at heights. Working at heights has many aspects for protection for example. You need to attach what's essential for protection training too. For example, you are in a construction company or in a small construction company that they are doing roofing. It's going to be that you'll need to find a goal that is going to support that small business is doing roofing in residences. It's not only to say you need this type of problem because you're going to comply, but the owner can tell, "How is it going to support to my business?" That's the thing; you need to provide an answer. You need to find that goal.

For example, a roofing builder needs to have working at heights training program. The efficiency and effectiveness of the roofing are going to increase the revenue and the professionalism of the company in doing this type of job. That means you comply; it's part of your job. The home's owner doesn't need to be worried about if someone can fall to the grass, then, he needs to deal with that injury or maybe a fatality. In the end, he would say, you know? I'm going to hire you because you have a good reputation in doing roofing in residence.

If somebody sees that your workers are not wearing the harness, you don't perform the job with quality. You don't treat your people with respect. That means you don't treat them your clients with respect. That's goal and a clear perception, in that opinion, it's going to increase revenue and efficiency. It's going to decrease cost and waste and it's going to support new products on the businesses that you have. Teaching a new or change production process, is something you need to apply too. If something is coming late, you'll need to design that goal of the training that is according to the business goal of the new process. Obviously, you're going to follow regulation, that's for sure. Your content of your training material is going to be according to regulation, that's a fact.

The problem here is that we believe that is everything. We train, we comply. It's not right; it is not. That perception has been in the industry for many years. As a result, safety violations have changed. Fatalities are still high and the lost time incident rate, at least in Canada it's still above one. In some provinces, it's above two. If it's this type of mentality and approach, you'll need to change your attitude. It's not only to comply, but it is to support the business.

Second Step

The second step is to determine the task the workers need to perform. Like I said earlier, you need to do an event or release of the task that they perform. You need to go with them, and you need to create some teams that are going to help you to develop that. There are all these training programs for the specific production line, for example, or in your business take one or two guys and then start asking them these types of questions because you need to have it. Also, you are going to identify the performance gaps between what your workers can do and what they're most able to do. Again, I'm going to present an example. You're working at heights in your roofing business, so I'm going to put to you this case. They don't wear a harness, well they're going to go slow. Why? They are not confident. They are taking care of maybe they're going to fall or not if they use the harness. Well, they won't fall, so they're going to do the job faster.

I'm going to give you another example. Maybe your company is not only providing roofing but also painting. To paint, you are using ladders to reach high spots or to assemble a scaffold? What is the safest way? If your workers are going to do scaffolding, you'll need to provide all the scaffolding training, right? That's the type of assessments you need. Not only training and I comply. I don't change anything that's going to be ladders and I'm in compliance. Yeah, before you miss the opportunity to find other ways to do the job more efficient, more effective, that at the end is going to impact your business. It's going to be faster, and it's going to be with quality. Now, you are giving your workers more tools and more ways to make him more capable of doing all the things with quality. It's going to benefit your business for sure.

Third Step

The third step is to determine the training activity that will help the worker learn to perform the task. Again, define the training activities that will help workers learn to perform the task. You need to identify what the workers need to do. You must recognize the training activities that will help them to learn to do those tasks. So, most of those training, especially in construction I would say, you'll need to do practical training as well. In manufacturing, it is also the same. I'm going to give you another example. You want to make people understand, especially in top management, understand what risk is, what is the hazard and what is essential to establish layers of protection, engineering, administer the PPE, a substitution or elimination. Explaining the concepts in a PowerPoint is good at the beginning. In the end, you don't achieve the goal. If you play the game, you'll design the game with dice. I haven't done that before.

They are going to understand in a better way what a layer of protection is, what an engineered layer of protection is, what a substitute layer of protection is; an administrator of protection and PPE.

People understands better the concept by playing, not by watching a PowerPoint presentation. You need to be creative on all those things. You can ask people. You can get on social media nowadays. Maybe you can ask, some of them are going to give you advice. That is the type of activities you need to have. Let me tell you something. You're going to continue with the PowerPoint presentation or speaking in front of a bunch of people. In adults, our span of attention is not going to be more than an hour. That's the best case. Nowadays, it's eight seconds because of technology. That's a fact. You'll need to find ways to keep people focused on the training and seeing the benefit.

You can do demonstrations as well. You can do many things depending on the topic. I'm going to give you another example, the fire extinguisher. We do have a controlled fire. Many people do that, but that's a prime example. You teach fire extinguishing and how to handle a fire extinguisher, fire theory, and basic stuff. Then, in the end, you go, and then you create a small fire, and you challenge the people to extinguish the fire. In many companies, this is a training, a fundamental training.

Fourth Step

The fourth step. You need to determine the characteristics of the workers that will make the training more effective. Here let's see You need to ask questions such as, are they more comfortable with computer based training or is the instructor leading the training? Or do they like self-guided or self-paced learning? Or do they like to play games? Or do they want to give ideas and then come up with a solution? You can help them from zero to design their safety program. It is the training program for that specific job or forth particular production line. You can train people, like the trainer trains. You can train some of them to keep the training.

When you blend some techniques, it's going to be a better way for you. Also, connect with the previous experiences with the new training materials. Always know when you're going to get updated and have those conversations. What's the needs for the update? It could be on a regular duty compliance or changing new equipment, some addition of new futures or parameters or something to the existing process. Always have those conversations. The best way to have these discussions could be a question that you have right now. Usually, I use something that's very common to process safety. It's management of change. What I would say is an excellent tool. Not only for controlling the changes and seeing all the aspects that are involved in that.

Also, as a communication tool, management of change is going to take something of the training that needs to be updated. The material needs to be updated. That change needs to be communicated. Also, in the discussions, use for example hazard assessment point of view and its risk-based approaches. You're going to see what type of risk in safety you are going to face. It's going to be the end of the result. What safeguards you have, what you need and what type of training you need to provide. In that session, the sessions you're going to has answered many questions. That's the information that needs to go to your training material. Now, we need to introduce concepts and ideas. Use metaphors, analogies, compilations. That's the reason why the study cases are the best tool for me, because you can create those metaphors, those ideas so you can open conversations.

Be receptive to all opinions and experiences because each member has their own experience and knowledge. Be susceptible to all. Sometimes you cannot satisfy everybody. At least listen to them and provide feedbacks. Sometimes, there are good ideas, but you cannot put it in place now because it could be a more significant project. You need more capital, you need more resources and you need time to develop that idea. Always be receptive. Then, explain why those ideas cannot be implemented now. Also, listen to people that have different opinions than the training. Be receptive in that. You need to control the group very well. Sometimes, I'm seeing in my experience, these type of conversations, they deviate to all the things. They are not for the forum to fix and to have that kind of discussions. It's good to listen but always keep track on the spot. That's the reason why study cases are perfect because you keep the focus on the people with the task, which helps in learning of the specific topic.

Also, it's good to learn ideas that do not match to the training because you can use them as well when you're explaining or responding to those, as the things you shouldn't do and the things that need to be done to prevent outcomes that you may not have under control. Incorporate the experience of your employees into your training program in the job. Coaching and mentoring programs, like I said, there is something that needs to be included. The coaching and the mentoring is the part of that we've always overlooked. Adding those two concepts, it will make your training program very successful, very efficient, and very useful because you are using the knowledge with experience.

You are using the experiences, some of them have a lot of experience, at about 25 years to 30 years in the company. That's the guys that are happy. They want to give something back to the company. Now, I think this is the perfect platform to let them do that. I love them to coach, I love them to mentor. Train those employees for coaching and for mentoring, it's worth it. It's an investment that you should do. Always provide ways to have feedback for the training. Have an evaluation of the instructor and you rank it from zero to five, the worst to the best, etcetera. Not only should it be what they think about the process or what they think about the training, it could be better, it could be worse too. Learn the ways, materials, et cetera. That will have enriched your program.

Being goal oriented is another characteristic. When we sit down, we expect useful information to come, so that we can use it right away. It's like when you buy something on the internet, a book for example. There is a reason why you are buying that book and spend the time to read it. It's because you believe the information that is on that paper and that book is useful to you. It could be in your personal life. It could be in your work. It could be in your professional development in many fields.

For example, the Isolation of hazardous energies for instance. That's a fascinating training course, if you do it in the right way., the training course won't focus only on lockout/tag-out. I will focus on how to identify those energies and how to isolate them. Lockout-Tagout can be one of the methods of isolation, but not the only one.

Putting people through a case study will expand their minds. It's not only going to be electrical, it could be genetics. It could be radiation, it could be pressure, it could be temperature, you never know. For example, forklift. How many hazardous energies are you going to find? At least 10, at least. Depending on the task that you're going to perform, and it could be more. You're going to be surprised. You do those type of examples, those kind of interactions; you compare of the course and after the class.

At the beginning of the course, you ask them to identify all the sources of energies. You make notes. At the end of the course, you ask the again how many sources of energy have you identified? You are going to see the difference. You're going to see more sources of energies identified at the end of the course. That's when the impact is coming. You say, "Okay, this course has helped me to identify those things. That's going to help me to identify those sources of energies on my work station." That's goal oriented.

If you're going to design activities, you might avoid that everybody gets bored. On this one, when you have your task inventory list and do a quick video or take pictures of the people who are going to get this training doing the job. That's task oriented. They are going to analyze that is already on that workstation in the production line. They are going to realize right away, that the information is going to help them.

The final goal of the training needs to be relevant and task oriented. You believe the material is going to help the worker and they're going to see your enthusiasm for how you are delivering that training material. How you are controlling the group and those conversations. At the end, it's a relationship between you as a safety professional or as a professional engineer. It's a business relationship, if they trust you, things are going to get better. How they're going to trust you, with open conversations, it's straightforward. Sometimes, they are wrong, and you need to explain to them why they are wrong. Always come to the discussion with information that you have. How you going to design the training material with these characteristics or consider these aspects.

We know that we need to comply with regulations, the regulation will change; therefore, you'll need to update the training material if necessary, and you'll need to explain why we need to follow that. It needs to be aligned with the business goals that we talked about at the beginning. Provide training with definite relation to the employees on their current job or the desired future job. This statement is significant because the mentality the company has, not regarding only those with safety that its risk-based oriented. Like you used principles a lot of the risk-based process safety that is focused on the risk, the outcome and how you are going to prevent it. How you're going for the risk studies, that call consequences to the cause and what is the safeguards to counter those effects. Then, you do the risk ranking, et cetera. You have that mentality.

Plan all the training materials as well, that's going to help you to design all the jobs in the future in the company. You're going to have better results, fewer headaches on getting the information going back and forth, get feedback from you and your final customer. That is going to be production, maintenance, warehouse, different departments. You need to have that open conversation. You'll need to have a strategic mentality and how you're going to solve that problem. There are problems with an outcome for a specific work station. If you go to the causes of that problem, it also applies other workstations. You say, "Okay, I'm in a converting area. Maybe, you can find that problem in the production line as well before converting." Then, you go backwards until you have opportunities to improve something else. That's the final goal of the training or one of the final goals. That training needs to solve a problem.

Always understand the human behavior. We cannot be sat down for long periods of time. After two hours, you lost complete attention. The training programs should be done in chunks, for example, no more than 45 minutes. For instance, I would say a flammable liquid training package in a chemical facility last around eight or nine hours or even more. You can create a CD with topics related to the handle and storage of these type of liquids with questions and interactive materials. The person who needs to take the training is going in chunks to assimilate all the content. She or he is going to learn in a practical matter. Include one of two cases of study as well.

Chapter 5
Learning Objectives

Before creating any training material or any training course, it's critical that you develop a list of learning objectives. The meaning of them is that the workers are going to be able to do that after their training is completed. Once you have created these learning objectives, you're going to build the content and goals to achieve the success of the training.

The rolling hill goes down, goes up, another peak goes down and goes up.

They are dominating in the top of the hill. They are establishing that training on daily basis of their activities, and they're going to master that. Once they go up, they are writing. It's steep, so you need more strength. You need to become stronger to achieve the second peak. You design another goal for the same training to master that little by little. That sometimes, you can use this analogy to plan refresh training. The other thing for developing objectives is to use the Monopoly game. How the Monopoly game is established. First, you buy some little houses, then, you buy some buildings, casinos and some properties. You also acquire, castles, countries and at the end, you dominate the world, right. That's the same with training; it needs to be done because we go from let's say I'm going to put another analogy.

You are riding your bicycle, and it's the first time. You're going to ride on a steep hill for 35 minutes. Good luck, I don't think you're going to achieve it, or you're going to make it. Not at all. You're going to finish sore and frustrated. That happens the same with the training. You need to chunk the training in different pieces. To make that content useful and second, less painful. Now you can create, you can add quizzes, tests, the case of studies, hands-on et cetera, to make that steep a little bit easier during the training. You're going to evaluate comprehension. Now, how are you going to assess that? One of the issue with objectives and goals is that we are either managers or trainers. In the industry, we have everything fast. We want everything that happens tomorrow or today or yesterday.

Training and assimilating the knowledge helps but understanding the knowledge is not the same. That's the reason why you need to also design objectives in the same training for coaching and mentoring. You need to define those. Imagine a new worker is facing a new environment, the guy is not going to absorb that knowledge right away. He needs to see, he needs to be observed. You need to develop those goals, and you need to prepare the mentor and the coaching system as well. The learning objectives they need to address the knowledge, skills, and attitudes that they need to build during that session or many sessions depending on what type of training you are delivering.

It's so important to go to the floor and share these learning objectives with people that have a lot of experience to get the feedback and verify if the fit with the current necessities and demanding from regulations and standards.

Remember, these objectives need to be specific, measurable, achievable, relevant and time-bound. When I say specifically, it's in the line of production or a task. When it's measurable, it is going to be in one month, two months, three months. How are you going to measure that knowledge acquired? When they said achievable, is it attainable to get everybody trained, mentor and coached in two or three months? That's something you're going to determine. The knowledge of the training is whatever is relevant to the position they will fill and time bounded are the same. Just that they need to know what's going to be the time to achieve that goal.

The learning objectives have some parts that you need to consider that it's the employee and their behavior. It's an employee, so who's going to be our audience? The skills and type of mentality that they have. It's not the same with a guy who's driving a forklift truck in the warehouse that is operating a line. That involves flammable or combustible liquids or combustible powders, different mentalities. Different ways to see things, the behavior that they have, the conditions under which they are working daily. The degree to which employees might perform the routine is significant, the degree of the employee must perform these activities.

You need to include rotation. You need to take in consideration layouts, activities, tasks that they are performing on that production line. Also, you can use lean manufacturing principles to design your learning objectives as well. It is essential to have these learning objectives reviewed by guys on the floor or whoever is going to be involved with the training and ask them if they understand them to verify if they are achievable, measurable and time bounded according to the job that they are performing.

Chapter 6
Training Materials.

Knowing how you're going to develop the training materials. It's critical. Improving the training material is like a steep hill. You have a team of cyclists they go up. Now, they're going to start climbing that mountain. In the group you have cyclists with 20 years of experience and cyclists with three months of experience. For sure, the cyclist of 20 years is going to climb faster than the three months. That is what happens in training too. You don't know when people are going to take breaks. You know that they are going to do it. That's the reason why you're going to develop training material in chunks because some are going to get tired faster than others, it depends on the skills, motivations, etc. You combine some PowerPoint presentations, some e-learning tools, some sessions with study cases, pictures, et cetera to analyze different situations. You're going to use all.

I recommend to creating your training in chunks because of the issues that you're going to face; other people learn faster than the others, you cannot do anything about it. The thing that you can do is to split the training. Also in training, take in count the five senses, they should interact. That means practice. You're going to do a respiratory protection training, so naturally practice with different masks, respirators. You're going to the feeling with different coverage. You're going to be explaining. I mean you're going to teach all the content of that, that's an example.

When you develop your training material, you need to consider five steps. The number one is preparing the goal, the audience, target the audience with this goal. Number two is to research a lot of information, and it should be accurate, mainly, on the technical side. Develop on the outline the best way to present the information to the workers as well. Write your draft to use and some employees, and there is a need to understand those words. Proofread and finalized.

Determine how the training needs to be. That's for technical writing or clinical training as well. Use best cases of topics and writing in the present tense, provide accuracy. Don't talk in the future mode, talk in the present. That's going to have a better impact on your training.

Some concerns will arise, there are two main concerns on development training. First, how you will help your employees to learn most efficiently; and number two, it is the learning objectives. You can use writing instructional materials. You can use the graphic designs, graphics for how to make your learning course or how you want to develop your e-learning.

It is essential to get a learning management tool to track schedules and completion of training.

The number two is the learning. What did they learn?

The number three is behavior, that's very important here. The training changed the attitudes, and it made them perform better and easier. That information contributes to the job, for them to work safer. The last is the results. Really, this training has helped to reduce incidents, to follow safety and other standards, such as safety standards. That's the type of information we need. The regulation can say you need to do that to comply, but the training has been sufficient to do that. That's something you need to check on when you perform evaluations. Also, you can create the assessments during the training to evaluate the learning objectives and that they conform to the training while they are getting the required information.

Company Information.

SAFEFFICIENT LIMITED is company which provides safety consultancy and engineering services located in Brantford On, Canada.

SAFEFFICIENT LIMITED offers the following services:

Process Safety Management:

I have helped organizations to implement and coordinate elements of the process safety management program to prevent outcomes such as fires, explosions or releases to protect the environment and public safety.

Health and Safety

I have helped companies to develop and implement health and safety programs and strategies to achieve legal compliance and incident reduction locally and internationally.

Safety Engineering.

I have helped operations to reach safety compliance in various stages of production, starts up operations, and equipment acquisition to comply with safety regulations, codes and standards to prevent the incident and protect employees.

You can contact me at www.pharma-chemicalsafety.com

About the author:

He holds the bachelor degree in chemical engineering from Iberoamericana University, Mexico City, Mexico.

He holds the P.Eng designation in the provinces of Alberta and Ontario, Canada.

He has 22 years of experience in the areas of Process Safety and Occupational Health and Safety.

 He has helped major companies in the pharmaceutical, chemical, food and manufacturing industries such as 3M Canada, Shering-Plough, Merck Sharp and Dohme, Champion technologies, CGGVeritas and Apotex Pharmachem Inc.to implement safety programs and reduce workplace incidents.

Achievements:

- **Health and Safety**
  - Achieved 70% reduction in potential hazards for laminator process and 100% elimination of injuries and near-misses at station by developing and leading Safety Kaizen Blitz.
  - Scored 97% on external audit and achieved highest score of any location in company by leading Certification of Recognition (COR) audit.
  - Achieved 50% reduction in safety incidents and 20% reduction in hazards within 6 months by creating and leading Hazard Recognition Program.

- **Pharmaceutical and Chemical Industry**
    - Impacted plant safety by leading development, planning and implementation of 7 of 14 elements of a process safety management program
    - Reduced dust by 100% and waste by 80% by leading the design of a Bio-Filter Project and specifications for new resin dump bag station
    - Developed strategy and implementation plan within three months of hire; presented requirements of the program to the Leadership Team and won initial approval
- **Consulting**
    - Drove hazard identification and risk-analysis for safety for two facilities with combined annual sales exceeding $80 million. Led multidisciplinary teams to identify and implement efficient and cost-effective solutions for safety-related issues in conformance with 3M policies and programs. Communicated project and program status to plant leaders and EHS management.
    - Provided technical advice on machine guarding, robot safety, and safety devices in accordance with CSA and ANSI standards for $1 million multi-robotic station.
    - Delivered safety technical advice for projects, including new ammonia storage tank and transfer technology of new products to facility.